40 Voices

A LENTEN DEVOTIONAL

Jean Wise

Healthy Spirituality Publishing
Edon Ohio
www.healthyspirituality.org

40 Voices - A Lenten Devotional

If you knew you were dying soon, would you see the people around you differently? Would you listen deeply to what they were saying? Would you observe their actions and behaviors, preserving their lives in your heart?

I wondered how Jesus considered all the people and places he spent time with during his last days. He knew the end of his human life neared. He knew exactly how the next few weeks would unfold. When Jesus interacted with someone, watched an event progress, or paused a moment to take the world all into his heart, aren't you curious what he was thinking?

We can gain insight to what Jesus experienced through the many voices in the story of his last week on earth. Jesus reached the edge of Jerusalem to face his final meal with his friends, the agony of betrayal, the trauma of unfair accusations, trial, and punishment, and then the finality of death. Everything ended until Easter morning when the entire world changed forever.

This major event transformed all who participated, reverberating through the centuries to our lives, changing the world forever.

The stories of the people and events surrounding Jesus in his last days hold wisdom for us today. We see our stories in their stories. We watch their struggles to trust God amidst confusing, conflicting circumstances. We see them wrestle in the murky times of waiting and discover hope when they emerge into the light of a new day. When we listen to their voices we imagine their world, their battles, and their lessons to light our life.

Jesus' presence in their story predicts his proximity within our story.

Lent is the season before Easter lasting 40 days, not counting Sundays. It is a time to reflect and remember our relationship with God. This time presents an opportunity for us to focus and draw closer to our Lord.

Lent offers the possibilities of giving up something we like to honor the sacrifice of Jesus' death and resurrection. People often choose not to eat chocolate or they limit their time on social media during these 40 days. One time, I gave up being sarcastic during Lent, quite a challenge for me. The practice of giving something back to God presents a way to open our hearts to God's transforming message.

Others reverse this practice in a more positive way by finding ways to give during Lent or reach out to others in unique ways. To assist in designating this time, many find praying more, writing hand-written notes of encouragement, and acts of kindness to be fulfilling.

Whatever you add or subtract from/to your Lenten journey, the point is to deepen your relationship with God. It is my hope this book of devotions accompanies you on this walk towards Jerusalem. As you hear the many voices and stories from Jesus' last week before his resurrection, I hope you see God's presence in your story.

Each devotion ends with an image, a question and a prayer. Gather symbols of your time with Jesus and place them near where you read each day. These items can be meaningful images from your own story, such as family photos or a representation of a significant spiritual event in your life. As another option, I suggest in each devotional, other images to gather reflecting that day's voice.

Use the questions and prayers to open your conversation with God about the lesson in that day's verse and narrative. Many find writing in a journal daily enhances their Lenten walk.

May you get to know God better. May his presence remind you how much he loves you. May your Lenten journey awaken new life in your soul

"And surely I am with you always,
to the very end of the age."
Matthew 28:20

Untying Our Knots

*As they approached Jerusalem and came to
Bethphage and Bethany at the Mount of
Olives, Jesus sent two of his disciples, saying to
them, "Go to the village ahead of you, and just as
you enter it, you will find a colt tied there, which no
one has ever ridden. Untie it and bring it here. If
anyone asks you, 'Why are you doing this?' say,
'The Lord needs it and will send it back here
shortly.'"
They went and found a colt outside in the street, tied
at a doorway. As they untied it, some people
standing there asked, "What are you doing, untying
that colt?"
They answered as Jesus had told them to,
and the people let them go.
Mark 11: 1-6*

I grabbed my favorite necklace to wear with my blue
sweater, only to discover that the chain jumbled in
several knots, kinks, and twists. What a mess. I
worked on the snarls for several minutes before
calling my hubby - renowned for getting knots out of
my jewelry. He has rescued me from myself more
than once in our marriage. Sometimes a gal needs a
little extra help.

One word jumped out to me as I sat and slowly read
the words from today's passage in Mark. This word
reminded me about how often I need help
straightening out, not just my jewelry, but my life.

Did you catch the word and related words that are
repeated five times in five verses? Five words all
linked to the word, untie.

I pay attention when a word is mentioned multiply
times and I open my heart to hear its lesson. When I

read the Bible, and see a pattern like this, I ask: What does this mean? Why does this word or phrase or image resonate in my heart? What is God inviting me to consider?

Jesus sent two of his disciples on a trip into town to find and bring back a colt for him. Jesus knew the colt was tied at a doorway. The disciples couldn't see it yet. They simply trusted, obeyed, and found the colt. They knew to look for this clue – a colt tied to a doorway. A repeated word is also a clue and an invitation to ponder.

"Untie it and bring it here" is Jesus' command. It is a wonderful statement to bring to our Lenten prayers. What Lord do you want me to untie and bring to Jesus this season? What do we need to unravel? What are we clinging to Jesus wants us to bring to him?

Jesus knows where our knots are located. He sees the sin that tangles our hearts. He understands the hurts to snarl our beliefs.

Sometimes getting a knot untied takes time and intention. Other times, I am surprised how easily I can disentangle the rope. Often I need extra help. But the result is freedom, being untied from what is holding me from being closer to God.

Guilt, fear, and discouragement tie us down. Worry and duties entangle us instead of bringing us delight. We hold fast to our grown-up gadgets such as cars and tech. We would rather cling to past hurts, than forgive and move on. It's easier to be sarcastic and to gossip than it is to care and make a difference. We are weighed down by how we used to do things instead of taking the risk to try something new.

The phase *"tied to a doorway"* echoed in my heart too. A doorway is a symbol for a transition. This image presents the question: What am I clinging to which is holding me back from taking the next step?

Jesus invites us to *"untie it and bring it here."* During Lent this year, pay attention to what traps you and what burdens you carry in your heart. What can we give up into Jesus' hands and let go? Freedom and love wait for us instead the weight of burden.

Jesus frees our tangled messes, unties our snarled sins, and sets us free.

Lenten Image: Piece of rope to untie

Question: What do I need to untie and give to God?

Prayer: Lord, take all my knots that intertwine my walk with you. I give to you my tangles, messes, and sins. Set me free, Lord.

Mount of Olives

When he came near the place where the road goes down the Mount of Olives, the whole crowd of disciples began joyfully to praise God in loud voices for all the miracles they had seen.
Luke 19: 37

The Mount of Olives surprised me on our visit to the Holy Lands. I am not sure how I envisioned it before, but not the steep, high mountain so close to Jerusalem. The bus brought us to the top of the hill to visit the Church of the Ascension where it is believed Jesus rose into Heaven. Then we walked the winding narrow road down towards Jerusalem. A panoramic view of the city loomed before us.

"We are on the Mount of Olives right now?" I asked incredulously. We sure were.

The 2900-foot Mount of Olives adds its voice to our Lenten journey. The two-mile descent into the Kidron Valley detailed the landscape, not just of Jerusalem, but also a view of Jesus' life too.

The small town of Bethany where Jesus found friends and refreshment sat about 1.5 miles to the east of this point. We paused on our walk at the place where it is said Jesus cried. At the bottom of the mountain waits Gethsemane, the location where Jesus prayed the night of his arrest.

The terrain loomed higher than I imagined. We walked the cobbled road that tilted unexpected in an extreme incline towards the Holy City. I always envisioned the Palm Sunday path flat or perhaps with a slight incline. I never anticipated this sharp angled road with its steep gradient.

The sheer incline of our descent on that road shouted a new insight to Jesus' last week. Our pace quickened as we walked down and I wondered how that little donkey kept his footing with Jesus riding on his back as people waved their palm leaves?

One of our fellow travelers lost control of her steps. She walked faster and faster down the sloop. We grabbed her arm to slow her down before she could fall. She was so relieved someone caught her and helped her stop before something tragic happened.

I wonder if Jesus looked at the faces of his disciples and the crowds cheering to ask himself who would help him face the coming events as his circumstances spun out of control.

Jesus also could see the large Jewish cemetery along the two-mile ridge to the left. People longed to be buried in that spot, as according to Jewish tradition, the Messiah will return, coming down the Mount of Olives into Jerusalem. Those buried there will be the first to see him.

White tombstones staked close together voice the hope and story of both death and resurrection.

Places hold meaning and tell the stories of our lives. The Mount of Olives heard Jesus pray and cry. The voices of those cheering, then betraying him reverberated on this mountain. This sacred place also witnessed Jesus' return to heaven.

During Lent, ponder the voices from the places in your life.

Image: Find a picture of the Mount of Olives and a place significant in your life's journey.

Question: How do the places in your life symbolize your life of faith?

Prayer: Lord, open my heart and eyes to learn the lessons from the Mount of Olives and the places in my life. Help me to see the landmarks you provide, guiding my way.

Hosanna!

A very large crowd spread their cloaks on the road, while others cut branches from the trees and spread them on the road. The crowds that went ahead of him and those that followed shouted, "Hosanna to the Son of David!"
"Blessed is he who comes in the name of the Lord!"
"Hosanna in the highest heaven!"
When Jesus entered Jerusalem, the whole city was stirred and asked, "Who is this?"
The crowds answered,
"This is Jesus, the prophet from Nazareth in Galilee."

Matthew 21: 8-11

Hosanna!

Not the most common word in our everyday language. I have said it during church services and sung it in hymns. I've read it in the Bible and heard it proclaimed on Easter morning. I assumed saying Hosanna praised the Lord and declared his glory. But I was wrong.

Hosanna differs unexpectantly in its meaning. This word originates from Psalm 118, verse 25 and is a cry to God for help. Hosanna expresses intense emotion imploring God to save us and save us now.

When the people waved their palm leaves and laid their coats on the path before Jesus as he rode into Jerusalem, they were asking him to save them. "*O Son of David, save us.*" Their shouts were cries for hope Jesus would free them from the tyranny of the Romans.

The Jewish people waited for centuries for the Messiah to rescue them and perhaps this man called Jesus was just the person to do the task they wanted.

They only saw their immediate need, while God has a much bigger plan in motion.

When I am stuck in the deep hole of discouragement and disappointment, I never imagine yelling, *"Hosanna."* My prayers for protection from fear and failure never voice this word either. When hurt drags you down and you feel lost and scared, is your response hosanna?

To me hosanna means praise. The word reminds me to keep my eyes on Jesus, my hope, anchor, and savior. I call out to the Provider, not to my problem.

Now that I know the meaning of this word, saying hosanna becomes an appropriate response to any difficult time and dark place. Hosanna gives hope, joy and help.

We are like those people lining the road on that Palm Sunday so many years ago. We cry for Jesus' help for our immediate need, failing to see God's bigger plan. Praise God in these times.

Hosanna!

Image: Palm leaf

Questions: How does hearing the word Hosanna now take on a different meaning to you?

Prayer: Lord, thank you for holding the entire picture in your mighty hands. When I call for help, when I shout Hosanna, you save me. Help me keep my eyes on you, not my problems.

House of Prayer

When Jesus entered the temple courts, he began to drive out those who were selling. "It is written," he said to them, "My house will be a house of prayer; but you have made it 'a den of robbers.'"
Luke 19: 45-46

Ever wonder why the scene at the temple upset Jesus that day? The people greeted him like a king with his arrival into Jerusalem. They cheered, celebrated, and waved palms. They bestowed a glorious, rousing parade in his honor.

Jesus' next stop brought him to the temple, the house of God, the home of his Father. Jesus deeply desired all people to be right with God. But he knew the truth before he entered the temple area.

Corruption existed throughout the temple of God. The stench of the animals, the exploitation of the money changers, and the filth, and noise of the rich taking advantage of the poor filled the air.

The custom of the day was to sell lambs and small birds for sacrifice. The experts in the law set up tables like a shop or bizarre. It was no longer the sacred space of God. The norm appears acceptable until someone comes along, drawing attention to the unsuitable.

The whole scene must have nauseated Jesus. Don't you love his passion to purify, restore, and correct the wrong? He reminded the people of Jerusalem this holy area was a house of prayer, not a resident for robbers.

This passage also reminds us we are the temple of God. In 2 Corinthians 6: 16 it says, For we are the temple of the living God. As God has said: *"I will*

live with them and walk among them, and I will
be their God, and they will be my people."

God is clear on this concept and Jesus is passionate
we remain pure, a temple, a house of prayer.

Lent invites us to consider what we need to clean
from our habits, behaviors and souls. What in our
lives needs to be restored to God's order? How do
we become as God intended us to be - a living house
of prayer?

We model our life after Christ. Jesus took the time to
draw away from the crowds and spend quiet moments
with God. We too can practice listening and being
with our Creator.

Prayer is the intimate communion with God. Ask God
to help you draw closer to him. Be willing to let go of
the clutter that doesn't belong in your temple to create
space for God to enter your heart. Make prayer a
priority. Become a house of prayer dedicated only to
God.

Image: Palms down, symbolizing surrender. Palms
up, representing faithfulness to your God.

Question: Does your temple need cleansing?

Prayer: Dear Lord, help me see the dirt, grime, and
corruption with the temple of my heart. Sweep me
clean, Lord, and make me a sacred space to welcome
you.

The Blind and Lame

The blind and the lame came to him at the temple, and he healed them.
Matthew 21: 14

I have a friend who doesn't come to our church anymore. She doesn't attend any church.

She still believes in God, but the institution where people gather to worship God has hurt, disappointed, and frustrated her. This makes me sad. We talk. I try to keep the bridge open to welcome her, and love and accept her. I hope someday church will be not a place that wounds her heart, but be a place of healing.

"The thing the church needs most today is the ability to heal wounds and to warm the hearts of the faithful; it needs nearness, proximity. I see the church as a field hospital after battle. It is useless to ask a seriously injured person if he has high cholesterol and about the level of his blood sugars! You have to heal his wounds.
Then we can talk about everything else.
Heal the wounds, heal the wounds. ...
And you have to start from the ground up."
Pope Francis

A church is a space for the imperfect, the ill, the hurting. As people of God, we are his church. Church is not just a building, but a collection of flawed and imperfect humans. An imperfect church filled with imperfect people.

We are called as God's church, not to hurt and turn away fellow pilgrims, but to be a place to heal, help, and accept. Our hearts provide the foundation to hold each other up, not tear each other down.

In the Jewish faith during Jesus time, the blind and lame were not allowed in the temple. They represented the broken, the imperfect, those considered unfit for God.

What did Jesus do? He turned the tables and welcomed all into his healing. He cleared out what shouldn't have been there to create space for those who should be invited into the presence of God. Jesus created a space of welcome. Jesus invited the imperfect, not the important.

The temple transformed into a house of God.

Ironic, isn't it? The Pharisees didn't see who Jesus was, but the blind and lame recognized him.

We are all wounded, damaged, and flawed. Our pews overflow with blind and lame people seeking acceptance and love. A space where wounds heal and all find wholeness and welcome.

In a world so torn apart by rivalry, anger and hatred, we have the privileged vocation to be living signs of a love that can bridge all divisions and heal all wounds.
Henry Nouwen.

Image: Band-Aid.

Question: How welcoming are you within church?

Prayer: Lord who welcomes all, help me recognize when I hurt and close off people different from me. Increase my awareness of those hurting and give me the wisdom to reach out with your love.

A Time for Rest

And he left them and went out of the city to
Bethany, where he spent the night.
Matthew 21:17

By the seventh day, God finished the work of creating the world. On the seventh day, God rested.

Today's verse points out Jesus also took the time to get away and to rest. Jesus leaves Jerusalem to travel to Bethany. He spends the night with friends. After the craziness of the triumphal entry into Jerusalem, the turmoil of clearing the temple of the money changers, and the energy expended in the healing of the blind and lame, Jesus needed rest.

Jesus also knew what events and emotions loomed in his future. Rest provided much needed self-care to restore and to build strength for the coming days. Going to Bethany also gave him the opportunity to reconnect with friends and with God.

Both God and Jesus model a healthy habit for us to follow. Take time for rest both before and after busy seasons.

A haven of rest can be a place, a companion, or a pause in time.

Bethany sits near Jerusalem and not far to walk for a break. Various commentaries explain the name, Bethany, represent *"the house of obedience."* Jesus left a defiant, unruly city to find a sanctuary of faith. Jesus sought a place of rest and intentionally made the time to go there.

Being with a friend also restores the spirit. Jesus knew his good friends, Lazarus, Mary, and Martha lived in Bethany. They understood, accepted, and loved Jesus – a welcoming, renewing environment to replenish the soul.

The time was imminent for events in Jesus' life. He intentionally took the time to journey to Bethany and to be with friends. We too, must manage the time in our schedules and calendars for retreat that offers rest.

I remember one summer when the kids were young and busy with their activities. My hubby worked his fulltime job and I was employed part-time. In my spare moments, I attended graduate school, completing my masters.

For two months, the summer before my last year of school, there were no classes. A little spare time in a crowded schedule unexpectantly appeared. We discussed what to do with the opportunity.

We planned a short family vacation. I decided to do something to rest and balance all the areas of my life. Physically, I scheduled a long overdue doctor's appointment. Mentally, I read on the backyard deck, enjoying a novel instead of serious college texts. Emotionally, I laughed and took leisurely walks. Socially, we enjoyed time with friends and I didn't worry about what wasn't being done. Spiritually, I wrote in my journal, prayed, and listened, and found rest.

Bethany represented the place of obedience where Jesus obeyed, listened to what he needed physically, mentally, emotionally, and socially. That summer became my Bethany. A time to get away and rest.

During Lent, ponder how you rest. Where do you go for respite and restoration? The place may be simply the chair where you spend time with God. The person may be the friend who listens and brings laughter into your life. The space on your daily calendar awaits to be discovered if you seek it.

Even in his hectic, daunting, and demoralizing last week on earth, Jesus took the time to rest. How about you?

Image: Hold your calendar for find time for rest.

Question: What is your Bethany?

Prayer: Lord of rest and restoration, we come to you for much needed respite. Help us find the place, the friends and the time to come away from daily living and to be with you for rest.

Who Do You Honor?

Yet at the same time many even among the
leaders believed in him. But because of the
Pharisees they would not openly
acknowledge their faith for fear they would
be put out of the synagogue;
for they loved human praise
more than praise from God.
John 12:42-43

"When I run, I feel God's pleasure."

I've always loved this quote from Eric Liddell. In 1924, Eric won the Olympic gold medal for Scotland in the 400-meter race. But he was supposed to compete in the 100-meter competition and never fully trained for the much longer 400-meter contest.

When Liddell arrived at for the Olympics he discovered the heats for the 100-meter dash were to be held on Sunday. A committed Christian, he refused to run on the Sabbath and withdrew from the race he was favored to win. He later entered the 400-meter which didn't involve time on Sunday.

The story goes that before the final, someone from the Olympic massage team handed Eric a verse from 1 Samuel that stated *"those who honor me, I will honor."*

Eric later explained *"The secret of my success over the 400-meter is that I run the first 200 meters as fast as I can. Then, for the second 200 meters, with God's help, I run faster."*

He also won bronze in the 200-meter race that year.

Eric ran for the pleasure of God. He didn't run for the praise of man. He knew God made him fast and he gave back to God the gifts God gave him.

After the Olympics, Eric returned to China as a missionary. During World War II, he remained in this service, even during the Japanese occupation. Liddell developed a brain tumor and died five months before liberation in 1945. It was revealed after the war that Liddell turned down an opportunity to leave the camp as part of a prisoner exchange program, preferring instead, to give his place to a pregnant woman. He served for the pleasure of God throughout his whole life.

In contrast, in today's voice from the Bible, John tells us the Pharisees "loved human praise more than praise from God."

The Pharisees were the teachers in Jesus' time. While most of them were not considered evil or bad men, their misguided intent and narrow beliefs drove their behavior. Their focus wasn't on God, but on obeying the law.

The Pharisees sought the praises from men, not from God. Who do we honor in our lives?

What do we live for? Where is our focus? Who is our God?

Image: Running shoes or a track medal

Question: Who do you honor in your thoughts, actions, and beliefs?

Prayer: I bow before you, Lord. You are who I seek to serve in all my heart, mind, and soul. Redirect me when I stray. Help me keep my focus only on pleasing and loving you.

Who were the Sadducees?

Some of the Sadducees, who say there is no
resurrection, came to Jesus with a question.
Luke 20: 27

Sadducees. I see this odd word and often glance right
over it, never fully understanding who this group of
people were in Jesus' time. This fun word to say
aloud, tickles the tongue on the way out of my mouth.
Sadducees.

Sadducees were a group of Jewish men, usually
wealthy and well connected, who influenced Israel
both politically and religiously. They fought to keep
their power by pleasing the Romans who occupied the
area at the time of Jesus. Their focus remained more
on the politics, than on religion.

The Sadducees did believe the holy scriptures,
especially the books from Genesis through
Deuteronomy. But they denied God being involved in
everyday life, and like the verse above shows us, they
didn't believe in the resurrection of the dead.

The Sadducees wanted to keep things as they were.
They viewed their role to uphold tradition and get
along with the current crowd. In other words — don't
cause waves. Keep things the same.

Apparently though, a few of the Sadducees wanted to
know more. This verse shows us some of them came
to Jesus with a purpose. Whether they wanted to trap
Jesus, expose him to get rid of him, or merely asking
to find out more about this prophet, they brought him
a question.

I love the rich heritage of traditions in the church.
Practices with ancient roots connect me to past and
future generations. Yet, we cannot cling so tightly to

the good old ways, that we miss the lessons found in asking questions.

Questions open us up to new possibilities and even changes in our lives. For example, take the risk and ask God what is important in our worship service.

Questions help us seek answers to our doubts and a clearer understanding of why we do things the way we do. One of my favorite questions is *"What does this mean?"*

Sometimes I admit to God, I just don't know. I am not even sure what or how to ask. A confusing situation, conflicting information, and false stories muddy my beliefs. I am learning to confess my lack of knowledge and trust the slowly unfolding wisdom of God to guide me.
Questions lift us out of our comfort zone and bring us face to face with the Comforter.

What a privilege it is, knowing we have a God we can approach with any type of question. He will answer. Our job is to be open, to listen and believe.

When the Sadducees approached Jesus, they called him *"teacher."* They put on the airs of being open, willing to listen and learn, and then as students are supposed to do, follow the instructions. Knowing what we know about the Sadducees, I doubt if Jesus' answer made much difference.

What do you call Jesus when you bring your questions to him? The answer may give you a hint of what type of answer you are seeking or whether you are truly ready to hear what wisdom and guidance God offers.

Bring your questions to God with an open and receptive mind and heart.

Image: Find an object that represents a teacher. An apple or a ruler?

Question: What difficult topics are you willing to bring to God?

Prayer: God of wisdom, often we don't know what to ask, or how to phrase the hunger, the confusion and the mess of our lives. Thank you for being willing to hear our struggles and questions and to help us hear your answers.

Jerusalem

As he approached Jerusalem and saw the city,
he wept over it.
Luke 19: 41

While in the Holy Lands, we visited many sites on the Mount of Olives. This mountain descends into the Kidron valley before the rise of the next hill where the city of Jerusalem sits. About half way down the steep mountain is the "Church of the Dominus Flevit."

This church received its name from the Latin words *"for the Lord wept."* Tradition tells the story that this is the location as Jesus approached his beloved Jerusalem, he cried.

Even the shape of the church speaks. Designed by Antonio Barluzzi, the building structure appears like a teardrop.

We entered the small chapel. The view from the window of this sacred space took my breath away with its panoramic scene of Jerusalem.

At first though, I didn't notice the looming golden temple as I peered through the arched-shaped glass into the holy city. What caught my attention was the symbols of the cross and the cup silhouetting the view. These ironwork images framed the landscape.

I almost missed the mosaic at the foot of the altar. I smiled seeing the image of a hen gathering her chickens under her wings, reflecting the verses from Luke 13: *"O Jerusalem, Jerusalem, you who kill the prophets and stone those sent to you, how often I have longed to gather your children together, as a hen gathers her chicks under her wings, but you were not willing."*

The city of Jerusalem stirred up deep protective emotions within Jesus, feelings that flowed with tears. Visiting this sacred spot opened my eyes to see Jerusalem as Jesus saw this holy city. He paused, knowing its fate and wept.

I too, felt tears well up in my eyes that day, not about Jerusalem, but with gratitude and joy knowing we have a Lord of deep, authentic, and eternal compassion. He feels what we do – sorrow over loss, grief over unnecessary destruction, and sadness over what might have been. He knows and understands us.

Jesus approached Jerusalem and saw her past, present and future.

Jesus also comes along side of us, knowing our past, present and future and loves us to the point of tears. Tears of great love.

Image: A teardrop, tissue to wipe tears.

Question: What brings you to tears?

Prayer: Loving Lord, thank you for your never-ending love, your deep compassion, and your willingness to protect us like a mother hen. We cannot begin to comprehend the depth of your love for us. Thank you.

It's All Greek to Me

Look how the whole world has gone after him!"
Now there were some Greeks among those who went
up to worship at the festival. They came to Philip,
who was from Bethsaida in Galilee, with a request.
"Sir," they said, "we would like to see Jesus." Philip
went to tell Andrew;
Andrew and Philip in turn told Jesus.
John 12: 19b-22

Digging into the Bible using our imagination often adds depth and colorful nuances to our insight from the scripture. Prayer using visualization is centuries old. St. Francis created the first nativity scene to help us see the people and setting of Jesus' birth. St. Ignatius encouraged his followers to use all their senses to bring alive the stories from the Bible.

In today's verses, we could become the Pharisee, or be Phillip or Andrew. But I am drawn to the Greeks.

The Greeks in this story were part of a regular crowd. They hadn't heard what caused the current turmoil. All they wanted to do was to worship at the temple.

Yet, people jammed the streets. The Greeks arrived in Jerusalem amidst noise, misinformation, and rumors of the Messiah. Who was this man? Is it true what people were saying? Could he heal and raise the dead? I can imagine their minds raced, their curiosity piqued.

They fought their way through the crowds to get closer. They actively sought out a special person to help them. They approached Phillip, then Andrew, as these two disciples had Greek names. Quite a Godcoincidence for them to find the right people in such a multitude of people.

The Greeks hungered for more. John never tells us what happened to the Greeks after this interaction, but being in the presence of Jesus is always life changing.

John also shares their voices to foreshadow that the good news of Jesus being here not only for the Jews — the entire world would soon know about Jesus. Today, the voices and stories invite us to seek and find the Lord.

Image: Alpha and Omega are the first and last letters of the Greek alphabet, represent Jesus as the beginning and the ending of all things.

Question: How are you seeking the Lord? What familiar voice helps you?

Prayer: Lord of all, you welcome everyone into your presence. Different languages, cultures, and backgrounds can find you. The hunger for you is deep and only satisfied in your presence.

Seeing the Invisible

As Jesus looked up, he saw the rich putting their gifts into the temple treasury. He also saw a poor widow put in two very small copper coins. "Truly I tell you," he said, "this poor widow has put in more than all the others. All these people gave their gifts out of their wealth; but she out of her poverty put in all she had to live on."
Luke 21: 1-4

I loaded the groceries into the rear compartment of my car. Glad to get out of the cold wind, I slipped into the driver's seat and turned on the engine. My mind already left the parking lot, racing to my next destination, and the finishing all the errands planned for the day. That is when the thought hit me.

Who checked me out? Yes, I did go through the checkout line. Yes, I did pay. But, did I look at the clerk? Male or female? Digging deep into my gray matter, I was thought it was a woman, but then again, I wasn't 100% confident of my answer.

I was so wrapped up in my to-do list, my getting things done, the accomplishments of crossing things off the list – I didn't see the live person in front of me. I treated her like she was invisible.

It wouldn't have taken any more time to smile, to connect, to whisper a prayer for her. My heart was blind. My observation skills and awareness of the present moment failed.

Jesus excelled in observation. He saw the little details and paid attention to the invisible.

One day Jesus watched the people putting money into the treasury. He sat down purposely to observe the busy temple scene.

The rich noisily let their coins clank into the treasury. Amazing though, Jesus noticed the widow putting in her tiny two cents in the box. Her gift represented the faith she had in God to provide for her needs. Her gift, a sacrifice.

What a lesson for us to follow. God's lessons surround us if we seek them with open eyes. Intentionally, Jesus observed and we are called to sharpen those skills also. Notice the details. Be aware of those in front of us.

Often this passage is used to preach about stewardship. That can be a great lesson, but the first four words of these verses lingered with me. "As Jesus looked up."

Let's do as Jesus does. Look up. Observe. See the invisible.

Image: Eye glasses

Question: Who is invisible in your world? How can you see them better?

Prayer: All-seeing Father, open the eyes of our heart to see what you want us to see. To recognize the ones you put in our view, so we may walk with them and help them.

Love is the Always the Answer

One of the teachers of the law came and heard them debating. Noticing that Jesus had given them a good answer, he asked him, "Of all the commandments, which is the most important?"
"The most important one," answered Jesus, "is this: 'Hear, O Israel: The Lord our God, the Lord is one. Love the Lord your God with all your heart and with all your soul and with all your mind and with all your strength.' The second is this: 'Love your neighbor as yourself.'
There is no commandment greater than these."
Mark 12: 28-31

Learning all the skills required to be an expert nurse can be overwhelming. The precise details of different instruments, procedures, and systems working together in the correct order is essential in providing good care. As a student nurse, I worried about doing everything just right.

As part of our education, we demonstrated in a lab setting various techniques under the guidance of our instructors. I still shiver remembering how nervous these skill assessments were for me. The number of items to memorize overwhelmed me.

One kind instructor though, gave us insight I will never forget. She taught us to see the whole picture. *"Pause first, and think,"* she advised. *"What is the underlying principle behind this technique? If you understand that, you will know what to do."*

For example, the rules of keeping a sterile environment stays the same no matter if you are applying a dressing, helping in surgery, or changing a catheter. Once I knew the core concept, the steps and details became clear.

The Scribes loved to discuss and study the details of the Jewish faith. They brought Jesus to the debate by asking him what is the most important commandment.

Jesus replied with the essential principle. Love God first. Then love your neighbor as yourself. Once you know and follow that guidance, everything else is evident.

Love is always the answer.

When we face a confusing, difficult situation, think about what is the loving thing we could do in our actions and words. When we don't know which way to choose, choose God first.

Of course, not all problems quickly or easily disappear even with this knowledge. But, if we discern with love, offer love, and take the first step with love, the path will emerge. When we treat others with love, love will heal and mend relationship.

Love is always the answer.

Image: heart

Question: What situations are you presently in that more love could help?

Prayer: Loving Lord, you draw us back, always reminding us to love first. Love you. Love others. Love ourselves. Keep our hearts ever focused on you, the source of this never-ending love.

Simon the Leper

While Jesus was in Bethany
in the home of Simon the Leper
Matthew 26: 6

I was minding my own business, looking at shoes in the department store when across the aisle a familiar voice shouted, *"Is that you, Seesholtz? Good ol' Sees?"*

Seesholtz is my maiden name. I haven't been called Sees since my college time, many more years ago than I will confess to in print here.

The 19-year-old still living inside me looked up, smiled, and responded to that familiar nickname like our pets react with enthusiasm at the sound of the food can opening.

Nicknames can be fun and endearing, but some carry the weight of ridicule and hurt, too. Many nicknames last a lifetime, seared into the memory of our hearts where we still respond even after many years. Names like Sees or Simon the Leper.

We don't know much about this character, Simon the Leper. Jesus spent a few days in Bethany during his last days on earth, visiting his good friends, Mary, Martha and Lazarus, and also having dinner at Simon's house.

Since Simon lived as part of that community, we assume he no longer had leprosy. I imagine Jesus healed him. But, still everyone called him Simon, the Leper. The name stuck, even though it no longer accurately described him.

Jesus heals all of us, too. He transforms our life and gives us new names. We are known now as beloved children of God.

Invite Jesus for dinner with you. Don't worry about the details. Put an empty chair at your table. Imagine the conversation. Let him heal you of past hurt and names that never fit the true person you are now.

We all carry the nicknames of our past within us. But God sees beyond them. God heals them.

Image: An empty chair

Question. What name were you called that you could give to God for healing?

Prayer: Healing Lord, thank you for being with us and making us whole. Come, stay awhile at our table, and let's enjoy our time together.

Extravagant Love from an

Alabaster Jar

While he was in Bethany, reclining at the table in the home of Simon the Leper, a woman came with an alabaster jar of very expensive perfume, made of pure nard. She broke the jar and poured the perfume on his head.
Some of those present were saying indignantly to one another, "Why this waste of perfume? It could have been sold for more than a year's wages and the money given to the poor." And they rebuked her harshly.
"Leave her alone," said Jesus. "Why are you bothering her?
She has done a beautiful thing to me.
Mark 14: 3-6

How do you define worship? When I think of deep authentic worship, my whole heart focused on my Lord, I think of the woman with the alabaster jar.

Jesus relaxed in Bethany over dinner. He knew what he would be facing the next few days. He watched his friends with the knowledge they would soon abandon and deny him, then passively watch him die. He also knew the outcome – the resurrection and God's good news of love and forgiveness spreading throughout the world.

But that night, Jesus received something *"beautiful."*

Alabaster is a precious stone found in Israel and used often in jars and containers to hold oils and perfumes. The thick walls prevented spoilage and evaporation. The only way to open the jar once sealed is to break the top.

In this account, the woman is unnamed, though some scholars think she may have been a prostitute or even Mary Magdalene. Who she is isn't as important as how she worshipped.

First, she approached Jesus with love, not allowing her brokenness and sin stop her from honoring her Lord. No one forced or commanded her to worship so elaborately. She simply turns away from her sin and enters love.

She surrenders her most precious object and pours it all out before and for Jesus.

She serves Jesus with passion, power, and devotion.

She sees to what Jesus needs, not asking for anything in return.

The broken woman brings her broken gifts to God and extravagant love makes her whole.

Our alabaster jars beat within us, holding precious perfume to be lavished on our Lord. Releasing all our hurts, blessings, and failure into God's forgiving hands lead to joyful extravagant praise and worship.

Come as you are, broken and ready. Take in the air brimmed with the fragrance of forgiveness. Feel the spirit embrace you as a child of God, accepted and loved. Healed and restored, allow worship to bubble up, overflowing in communion with our Lord and Savior.

Come, bare and vulnerable, worshiping until tears spill onto Jesus' scarred feet.
Come, sinful, broken, and weeping.
Break open your past and give your heart, your alabaster jar to Jesus.

Image: Jar of perfume or oil

Questions: What do you cling to, afraid to give back to God? What do you need to shatter which blocks you from fully worshiping him?

Prayer: I come, Lord. I bow down before you, offering my life, my tears, my fears, my all. Take the broken pieces of my heart, given to you in faithful worship, and create your masterpiece.

Choices

Now the Festival of Unleavened Bread, called the Passover, was approaching, and the chief priests and the teachers of the law were looking for some way to get rid of Jesus, for they were afraid of the people. Then Satan entered Judas, called Iscariot, one of the Twelve. And Judas went to the chief priests and the officers of the temple guard and discussed with them how he might betray Jesus. They were delighted and agreed to give him money. He consented, and watched for an opportunity to hand Jesus over to them when no crowd was present.
Luke 22: 1-6

Williams Jennings Bryan wrote our "*destiny is not a matter of chance; it is a matter of choice.*"

I often wonder about Judas and his choices. Why did he betray Jesus? Why did he betray his friend to the highest bidder for pieces of silver? What if he, instead of choosing suicide, Judas asked for forgiveness? That choice may have led many more people to follow Christ. What if Judas chose differently and his legacy became a powerful story of forgiveness and grace?

Jesus knew what Judas was going to do that night and yet, Jesus still washed the feet of his betrayer. What an example of love.

Judas still betrayed Jesus. He could have changed his mind. He could have asked forgiveness. He could have lived, telling others how much God loved him, forgave him, and changed his life.

Choices. We all make some good ones and in moments of confusion, fear and despair, choose wrongly. How do we live with all the decisions that end up determining the direction of our lives?

Some detours in life are not of our own choosing.

We didn't pick our parents. We didn't decide to have cancer attack our bodies or take the lives of our loved ones. We didn't choose to have the factory close or the car to break down at the worse possible financial time.

How we react to life's circumstances is our choice.

We also can admit our failure, confess our sin, change our ways. Too often pride, the desire for power, and wanting to keep the illusion I am in control, draws me away from God. I wonder if pride stopped Judas from coming back and asking for forgiveness.

Lent is a time for us to face our bad choices in life and return to God asking for forgiveness. We are welcomed to come back over and over again.

God loves us no matter how well or poorly we choose the direction of our lives. He waits, willing to forgive even the most hideous act of betrayal. We can turn and run to him. The choice is ours.

Image: A silver coin

Question: What blocks you from coming to God for forgiveness?

Prayer: Forgiving Lord, we come once again, knowing our sin, knowing we failed. Thank you for accepting us, loving us, and forgiving us.

The Upper Room Hospitality

Say to the owner of the house he enters, 'The Teacher asks: Where is my guest room, where I may eat the Passover with my disciples?' He will show you a large room upstairs, furnished and ready. Make preparations for us there."

Mark 14: 14-15

We were running late. The traffic crawled along the turnpike following a major accident. I was anxious to arrive at our hotel. I called ahead to be sure they had our reservations and knew we were coming. I didn't want them to give the room to someone else on this busy holiday weekend.

The voice at the other end of the phone politely replied all was ready and waiting for us. They had warm cookies baked and put the extra pillows I requested in the room. *"Don't worry. We have the room prepared for you,"* she said.

She even offered to tell the hotel restaurant to stay open later in case we needed supper.

Jesus too, prepared ahead for a special meal with his friends, his disciples. These verses imply when he sent them into Jerusalem, he directed them to a specific person to finalize the plans.

Jesus holds our future and has already made our reservations. He prepared the place for us as he foretold in John 14. Our reservations are in place.

Jesus created a space for us to come to him. He demonstrated for us holy hospitality.

I have always liked Henri Nouwen's definition of hospitality:

> *Hospitality means primarily the creation of free space where the stranger can enter and become a friend instead of an enemy. Hospitality is not to change people, but to offer them space where change can take place. It is not to bring men and women over to our side, but to offer freedom not disturbed by dividing lines.*
> *Henri Nouwen*

Hospitality is a mindset of generosity and creates an environment where a person feels accepted, wanted, and loved. It is unselfishly serving others in a warm and friendly manner.

A friend told me she loves hospitality because it gives her delight to anticipate the needs of others before they even realize it. She related it to being a good waitress and filling up the water glass before it was empty or providing extra napkins. Then she added. *"It's how God treats us."*

We cultivate this welcoming spirit by opening the space in our hearts and our lives, to invite others in, to walk/companion others, and to care for others. Welcoming requires paying attention and being present. We can all learn and practice Upper Room hospitality as Jesus did.
Someday Jesus will welcome us home, to the place he has prepared for us.

He may even have warm cookies waiting for when we arrive.

Image: Welcome mat

Question: How can you practice hospitality this Lenten season?

Prayer: Welcoming Lord, you so generously prepared a place for us. Thank you for showing us how to welcome others though your love and hospitality.

Lessons from Gethsemane

*Then Jesus went with his disciples to a place called
Gethsemane, and he said to them, "Sit here while I
go over there and pray." He took Peter and the two
sons of Zebedee along with him, and he began to be
sorrowful and troubled. Then he said to them, "My
soul is overwhelmed with sorrow to the point of
death. Stay here and keep watch with me."
Going a little farther, he fell with his face to the
ground and prayed, "My Father, if it is possible,
may this cup be taken from me. Yet not as I will, but
as you will."
Then he returned to his disciples and found them
sleeping. "Couldn't you men keep watch with me for
one hour?" he asked Peter. "Watch and pray so that
you will not fall into temptation. The spirit is willing,
but the flesh is weak."
He went away a second time and prayed, "My
Father, if it is not possible for this cup to be taken
away unless I drink it, may your will be done."
When he came back, he again found them sleeping,
because their eyes were heavy.
So he left them and went away once more
and prayed the third time, saying the same thing.
Matthew 26: 36:44*

On our trip to Israel we walked in the garden of
Gethsemane. Olive trees lined the garden path.
These trees thrive in the Holy Lands and every meal
we ate offered at least one form of olives. Olive oil
and olive wood gifts decorated the shelves of stores
we visited. We passed miles of olive tree groves.

Olive trees don't grow in northwest Ohio where I
live, so I knew little about this tree. But, it was
something our tour guide said that resonated within
me and caused me to listen more closely to
the lessons from the olive trees.

George told us olive trees could grow in any type of soil and had shallow roots. With this limited root system, it was best to plant the trees near the bedrock so their roots could wrap about the solid foundation and be able to withstand the wind and storms.

Not a bad image for us spiritually, too. I like the thought of digging deeper, clinging to the true Bedrock for my foundation.

Did you know some olive trees in Israel are estimated to be 100, and even 2000 years old? The trees we saw in the Garden of Gethsemane weren't that old, but did grow from the base of the old trees that may have been there from the time of Jesus. They are virtually indestructible; even when they are cut down, new life will grow back from the roots.

Olive trees can remain productive as long as they are pruned correctly and regularly. The crop from old trees is sometimes enormous, but they seldom bear well two years in succession, and in many cases, a large harvest occurs every sixth or seventh season. Olive trees give me hope and encouragement in time of pruning and seasons of rest. They also remind me we are called to bear good fruit our entire lives even as we grow older.

Olive trees are not impressive, like the giant oaks or majestic redwoods. Their gnarly twisted trunks with their short squawky stature seem ordinary and even ugly at first. But think about their strength and endurance – lasting for so long. What beautiful wood appears with the work of the Master.

The olive branch is the symbol of peace. We walked past the word "PEACE" spelled out with white stones in the Garden, during our candlelight processional our last night in Jerusalem.

That Thursday evening, we attended a peaceful liturgy in the Church of All Nations. We came there to pray, just as Jesus came to that sacred location to spend time with his father. Bible verses were read in different languages followed by silence, then chanting.

We then walked outside to proceed around the olive trees lit only by the moon and soft candlelight. Ironically, as we quietly chanted our praises to God on this holy ground, each of us carrying a glimmering candle, we could hear gunshots by the near Temple Mount area. This experience deepened my commitment to pray for peace in this blessed and wonderful part of God's creation.

What did Gethsemane teach Jesus? Teach us? When you get the opportunity, take a walk in the woods. Look at the trees and ask them to teach you something God wants you to learn. Listen to the lesson.

Image: Olive oil or something made from wood from an olive tree

Question: What lessons does wood – from trees and from the cross – teach you?

Prayer: Master Creator, you teach us lessons if we only listen and pay attention. Help us learn what you want us to know today and every day.

Peter

So he (Jesus) got up from the meal, took off his outer clothing, and wrapped a towel around his waist. After that, he poured water into a basin and began to wash his disciples' feet, drying them with the towel that was wrapped around him.
He came to Simon Peter, who said to him, "Lord, are you going to wash my feet?"
Jesus replied, "You do not realize now what I am doing, but later you will understand."
"No," said Peter, "you shall never wash my feet."
Jesus answered, "Unless I wash you, you have no part with me."
"Then, Lord," Simon Peter replied, "not just my feet but my hands and my head as well!"
John 13: 4-9

Peter is one of my favorite Bible characters. I love his passion and enthusiasm. I see my own human mistakes and my constant requests for forgiveness mirrored in Peter's life. Peter gives me hope.

I smile at the impetuous Peter. At times, he is rash, hot-headed, and spontaneous. He is ready to leap right into Jesus's ministry with his sudden obedience, while struggling internally with still wanting to do things his way. He quickly defends Jesus by cutting off the ear of the soldier arresting his Lord, and a few hours later Peter denies ever knowing Jesus.

Peter bravely steps out of the boat to walk on the water with Jesus, but then takes his eyes from his savior, and sinks. Jesus reaches out to save him.

At the last supper, Peter resists Jesus washing his feet, until Jesus tells him it is part of the journey with him. Immediately, Peter changes his mind and offers his full self.

Rejecting, failing, learning, changing, starting over – sounds like life, doesn't it? God knows and understands this human journey we share comprises of many twists, turns and blunders.

When a toddler begins to walk, he falls frequently, yet the parent encourages and cheers him onward. The little one giggles and gets up to try again. The delight of learning this new skill brings joy both to the child and the parent.

I believe God delights in walking along side us in all our adventures, miscues, and detours. Peter demonstrates this truth.

Peter's story gives us hope.

Hope that I too, can demonstrate when I fail, but not give up.

Hope that when I betray or let down my Lord, I know God forgives and welcomes me back.

Hope in my dark doubts that with faith we acknowledge who God is, who Christ is, and know how deep our desire is to love and serve them.

Jesus uses even the most questionable characters, those who mess up, those of us who continually fail, those of us who fall short of our good intentions. He accepts us, and sees us through the eyes of his heart as children of God, even though we fall like toddlers.

In every instance, God offers us forgiveness, love, and smiles with delight as we learn to walk in his ways.

Image: Picture of a toddler

Question: What failure has taught you a great lesson?

Prayer: Father God, thank you for standing by our sides and encouraging us in this walk of life. Your opens arms are ever present to receive us, lift us up, and set us on the right path.

John the Beloved

"Woman, here is your son…. Here is your mother"
From that time on, this disciple took her
into his home.
John 19:26b, 27b

Who do you entrust with your most valuable possession?

When we began having children, we cringed at the thought of what would happen if we died? Who would care for our kids? Who would raise them the way we wanted?

Sometimes, a family member is the best choice. We had to consider the factors of where do they live and were they close to other family members? Would that couple love our children and foster the values and experiences we wanted?

Sometimes, a close friend is another option. Someone you know, trust and would represent you in that relationship without hesitation.

Jesus was dying. He looked down and saw his good friend, John. Jesus trusted and loved John and gave him a huge responsibility to care for someone Jesus also loved.

"Woman here is your son. Here is your mother."

That exchange must have given Jesus comfort and peace. He knew his mother would be cared for and placed her into good hands.

In these last moments of his life on earth, Jesus cared for someone else. In the midst of suffering and dying, the needs of those he loved mattered. This truth reveals the depth and width of how much God loves each of us, and will care for us even more now in the power of his resurrection.

Jesus called John, his beloved friend. God calls us his beloved children. He protects us and provides for our future care. God holds our lives and the Holy Spirit guards our paths.

We are God's most valuable possessions.

Image: A set of legal papers representing an adoption.

Question: What is your most valuable possession and how do you plan to protect it?

Prayer: Loving Father, we are amazed at the depth of your love and protection. To be called beloved children of God brings life and hope to our days. Thank you!

Sons of Thunder

These are the twelve he appointed: Simon (to whom he gave the name Peter),17 James son of Zebedee and his brother John (to them he gave the name Boanerges, which means "sons of thunder"), 18 Andrew, Philip, Bartholomew, Matthew, Thomas, James son of Alphaeus, Thaddeus, Simon the Zealot.
Mark 3: 16-18

What is your name? How did you get your name? This is always a fun question to ask others. There is always a great story.

Many of us are named after someone in the family or even a celebrity. Some parents creatively combine names to create new one. Others gain their name because the parents like the sound mixed with a middle and last name.

Jesus knew the names of those who followed his ministry and walked with him that last week on earth. He even changed names; calling Simon, Peter and James and John, the Sons of Thunder.

Ever wonder why Jesus called the brothers by that nickname? Scholars don't know for sure, but these were two strong men, physically fit outdoors men. I imagine them like the rough cowboy type, ready for battle and not willing to step aside.

Thunder implies loud booming voices. I bet they let their opinions be known and loved to debate the scriptures, and what the future may hold for the ministry of Jesus.

Thunder also explodes unannounced. We aren't sure when the next blast will rumble from the clouds. We can't control or manage thunder, but God can.

God knew James and John, these Sons of Thunder. He shaped rough, unruly and willful men into obedient followers of Christ. The first apostle martyred was James.

John's new name became the one Jesus loved and wrote scripture centered on love. This Son of Thunder composed one of the best-known Bible verses:

For God so loved the world that he gave his one and only Son,
that whoever believes in him shall not perish but have eternal life.
John 3: 16

God knows our names, too. He may even have a loving nickname in his heart describing our temperament. Consider how God shaped his followers, and through the power of the Holy Spirit continues to form us today.

Image: Nametag

Question: What nickname based on your personality do you think God may call you? How is God using that temperament to shape your walk with him?

Prayer: Creator God, you continue to form, guide, and mold us today. May we be open, pliable and willing to be like clay in your Sculptor hands.

Annas

Then the detachment of soldiers with its commander and the Jewish officials arrested Jesus. They bound him and brought him first to Annas, who was the father-in-law of Caiaphas, the high priest that year Then Annas sent him bound to Caiaphas the high priest.
John 18: 12-14, 24

How do you want to be remembered? What type of legacy will you leave?

Today's voice from Jesus' final week is a man called Annas. Annas appears four times in the scriptures. In his younger years, he served as the high priest and now his family carried on the tradition. His son-in-law is Caiaphas was the current high priest when Jesus was arrested.

What did the high priests do? These ruling priests officiated over the religious life of the Jewish people and served as judges. High priests were appointed for life, but often they passed the title onto a relative. Though no longer serving as the current high priest, Anna probably still held powerful influence over decisions.

Annas is mentioned as John the Baptist started his ministry "during the high priesthood of Annas and Caiaphas." But history doesn't tell us much more about this voice.
After Jesus's arrest, the soldiers though, brought Jesus first to Annas. I wonder if he gave the order to arrest him or the soldiers knew of his influence.

Note the scripture points out Annas didn't just send Jesus to Caiaphas, he sent Jesus as a prisoner, bound, and shackled.

At this point in Jesus' last week, he is known as a prisoner, arrested, and on trial. Annas is recognized as an influential judge.

Often we are known for our roles, the jobs we held, even after retirement. *"He was my teacher." "You know her, she ran the grocery story uptown." "She is a nurse."* They are all labels others bestow on our identity.

How do you want to be remembered? How will others describe you later in life?

Jesus' true identity, though not visible yet, is the Messiah, the Son of God. Annas is a minor character passing judgment on an innocent man.

And our true identity? A Child of God.

Image: A mirror

Question: Look at your reflection and consider your legacy.

Prayer: Lord, you made us, wired us, created us as we are. Thank you for continually forming our hearts, guiding our ways, and helping us discover our true value as your children of God.

The Courtroom of the Sanhedrin

They took Jesus to the high priest, and all the chief priests, the elders and the teachers of the law came together. Peter followed him at a distance, right into the courtyard of the high priest. There he sat with the guards and warmed himself at the fire.

The chief priests and the whole Sanhedrin were looking for evidence against Jesus so that they could put him to death, but they did not find any. Many testified falsely against him, but their statements did not agree.

Then some stood up and gave this false testimony against him: "We heard him say, 'I will destroy this temple made with human hands and in three days will build another, not made with hands.'" Yet even then their testimony did not agree.

Then the high priest stood up before them and asked Jesus, "Are you not going to answer? What is this testimony that these men are bringing against you?" But Jesus remained silent and gave no answer.

Again the high priest asked him, "Are you the Messiah, the Son of the Blessed One?"

"I am," said Jesus. "And you will see the Son of Man sitting at the right hand of the Mighty One and coming on the clouds of heaven."

The high priest tore his clothes. "Why do we need any more witnesses?" he asked. "You have heard the blasphemy. What do you think?"

They all condemned him as worthy of death. Then some began to spit at him; they blindfolded him, struck him with their fists, and said, "Prophesy!" And the guards took him and beat him.

Mark 14: 53-65

Imagine a courtroom. The tall beams support the high ceiling. Voices echo, bouncing between cold stone walls. The crowd of spectators bristles with whispers and jeers.

Before us sits the panel of judges ready to interrogate the one arrested. More than 70 priests assemble in a half circle peering down from the gallery on the lone perpetrator standing on the side. He stands, looking defeated, with hands tied behind his back and legs in chains. No defense lawyer is present.

The testimony begins with the first, then second witness.

"He said he would destroy our church! And in three days make a new one."

"Yah, build a whole new church without the help of human hands."

Another reports different and conflicting accusations.

The judges, the Sanhedrin, begin their interrogation.

"Are you not going to answer? What is this testimony these men are bringing against you?"

Jesus remains silent.

"You are accused of being a false prophet. Say something!"

The high priest leans forward, asking, "Are you the Messiah, the Son of the Blessed One?"

"I am," answers Jesus.

"See, he confesses. He thinks he is the messiah. What is your judgement?"

"Condemn him!"

This Jewish court system was called the Sanhedrim which means "sitting together." This council, consisting of 71 priests, elders, and scribes ruled on cases and even had the power to condemn and pass death sentences. They were the prosecutors and judges at Jesus' trial.

As you witness this hearing, who are you in that room? The judges? A witness? Part of the lurking, curious crowd on the sidelines?

No one rose to Jesus' defense. Not one person.

Who in your life today is defenseless?

Image: A judge's gavel

Question: Who is voiceless in your world you can speak for and defend?

Prayer: God of all people. Deepen within our hearts a compassion for those without help, protection, and defense. Clear our ears to hear the cries of the voiceless and give us courage to reach out and help those in need.

Caiaphas –A Holy Hunch from an Unholy Hypocrite

Then one of them, named Caiaphas, who was high priest that year, spoke up, "You know nothing at all! You do not realize that it is better for you that one man die for the people than that the whole nation perish."
He did not say this on his own, but as high priest that year he prophesied that Jesus would die for the Jewish nation, and not only for that nation but also for the scattered children of God, to bring them together and make them one. So from that day on they plotted to take his life.
John 11: 49-53

As the current high priest, Caiaphas held many responsibilities. He served as the chief justice for the Sanhedrin, the council that ruled on various court cases. He also controlled the money exchanged at the temple and oversaw the all the personnel working there. This was on top of performing his priestly duties and rituals.

One busy man who also had to keep the peace between the Jewish people and their Roman rulers. Serving as a liaison, he kept both sides happy – not an easy endeavor.

Caiaphas and the Sanhedrin make appearances throughout the gospel stories of Jesus. After the celebration of Jesus raising his friend, Lazarus from the dead, the council discussed how to best deal with the *"problem of this man called Jesus."*

They began to conspire for his death.

But as today's verse reveals, Caiaphas makes a prediction – one he had no idea how right he was and how profoundly his prophecy would impact the world.

"Let one man die, instead of a whole nation," offered Caiaphas.

Caiaphas suggested one person be sacrificed for all.

Caiaphas didn't know how true his word foretold the future.

God knew.

Image: Hold your calendar and listen to God's prediction for your future.

Question: When has your intuition foretold your destiny?

Prayer: Almighty God, you hold the future and know all the details of coming events. Help us hear your hints when we need to know and obey, even when we have no idea what is coming. You are the light of our path and we want to follow only you.

Barabbas

Now it was the custom at the festival to release a prisoner whom the people requested. A man called Barabbas was in prison with the insurrectionists who had committed murder in the uprising. The crowd came up and asked Pilate to do for them what he usually did.
"Do you want me to release to you the king of the Jews?" asked Pilate, knowing it was out of self-interest that the chief priests had handed Jesus over to him. But the chief priests stirred up the crowd to have Pilate release Barabbas instead. Wanting to satisfy the crowd, Pilate released Barabbas to them. He had Jesus flogged,
and handed him over to be crucified.
Mark 15: 6-11, 15

Ever have a decision backfire?

You map out all the details to seal a deal. You plot its course and put the steps into action. Your offer will be so appealing, no one will turn you down or choose an alternative.

Then the impossible happens. People decide the opposite choice from your well-conceived proposal.

Pilate imagines he knows the outcome of that day. The prisoner, Barabbas, assumes the conclusion will be his death.

A prisoner release occurred each year as one of the rituals during the feast of Passover. An action what was supposed to spread good will and keep the Jewish people happier under the rule of the Romans.

Pilate has two choices to offer the Jewish crowd. The innocent man called Jesus or the murderer and criminal Barabbas. One of them would be crucified - the guiltless one or the guilty one.

Pilate presumed Jesus would be set free, saving him the trouble of condemning the man.

The plan backfired. When given the choice, the crowd wanted Barabbas freed. Never in his wildest dreams, did Pilate conceive this action.

Neither did Barabbas. Imagine his shock hearing the news.

The Bible never tells us what happened to Barabbas. I wonder if he ran back to his former life of crime.

Or maybe he lingered in the crowds and watched Jesus lug the cross through the streets of Jerusalem. Did he observe the crucifixion of Christ, feeling the earth quake at the moment of his death? Did he think – that should have been me on that cross, not him?

Did the cross change Barabbas? Abruptly, his life was offered a new course, a new chance, an opportunity for a fresh beginning.

Because of the Lord's great love we are not consumed, for his compassions never fail. They are new every morning; great is your faithfulness. Lamentations 3: 22-23.

Every new day brings this same opportunity for a fresh beginning for us, too. Will the cross change us?

Image: A cross

Question: How does the cross change your life?

Prayer: Lord, you sacrifice all for us to have eternal life. Break down the barriers of our hearts so your presence transforms us as you called us to be.

Pay Attention to Your Dreams

While Pilate was sitting on the judge's seat, his wife sent him this message: "Don't have anything to do with that innocent man, for I have suffered a great deal today in a dream because of him."
Matthew 27: 19

My husband's pet peeve is about driving on a busy four-lane highway with construction ahead. Several miles before the road work, all the drivers see the same sign stating "right lane closed ahead." All the drivers know the drill: merge from two lanes into one.

My husband follows the rules. He moves the car over to the open lane early. Then he gets angry. Car after car races by, waiting till the last possible moment to squeeze into the line of traffic in the open lane.

"Didn't they see the sign? The warning?" he growls.

Pilate also received an early warning about Jesus. His wife sent him advice about condemning the innocent man. Her dreams told her trouble would mount if he sentenced Jesus to death.

I am the type not to remember my dreams. I have learned though, that the more you practice remembering them, writing them down immediately upon waking, you remember more details.

The Bible contains many cautions arising from dreams. Twice predictions originating from dreams impact Jesus' life.

At the birth of Jesus, wise men from the East followed the star to worship the newborn King. Not sure where to find him, they visited Herod to seek information about the King's location.

The threat of a king being born disturbed Herod who asked the wise men after they find this king to return to let him know where the king now lived so "he can worship the new king too."

After they find the baby Jesus, the Magi are warned in a dream not to go back to Herod, but to go home another route. The Magi listened to their dreams.

Joseph soon is also warned in a dream to leave Bethlehem and escape to Egypt in order to avoid the wrath of Herod.

Two dreams warned. Two precautions heeded.

But Pilate decided to listen to the crowds, and not his wife.

I wonder what conversation those two must have had after the crucifixion and Jesus' resurrection.

Dreams, intuition, listening quietly to God – all offer us direction and clearness when discerning a decision. During Lent, pay attention to your dreams. Be still and listen for the voice of God in your prayers, reading, and quiet time.

God is always present. All we need to do is open our eyes and heart to notice him.

Image: A small notepad by your bed to keep track of your dreams

Question: What will help you listen for guidance when discerning a next step?

Prayer: Lord of our day and nighttime dreams, dreams are a gift from you. Help us hear your lessons in all our experiences with you.

Pilate

Pilate had a notice prepared and fastened to the cross. It read: Jesus of Nazareth, the king of the Jews. Many of the Jews read this sign, for the place where Jesus was crucified was near the city, and the sign was written in Aramaic, Latin and Greek. The chief priests of the Jews protested to Pilate, "Do not write 'The King of the Jews,' but that this man claimed to be king of the Jews."
Pilate answered,
"What I have written, I have written."
John 19: 19-22

When parents name their children, one aspect of choosing the right name is writing out the baby's initials. They might want to avoid letters spelling words such as ROT, COW, or GAS.

Our initials become part of our identity. We break apart the name to form something new. We use them on monograms and sweaters. We know famous people just by the letters from their name: JFK or FDR.

Even brands use initials as shortcuts for their names: A&W, M& M. We probably don't know the full names of some famous authors, just their initials, as in J.R. R. Tolkien and e.e. cummings.

And many of us remember ET and wondered *"who shot JR?"*

Initials identify us and communicate a truth. Initials become a caption for others to remember our story.

Pilate had a sign fastened to Jesus' cross. Today's verses tell us the words proclaimed: *"Jesus of Nazareth, King of the Jews."* He mocked the Jewish people, laughing that only they would have a pitiful dead king like Jesus.

To make matters worse, Pilate took the words, King of the Jews, and transcribed them into three languages: Hebrew, Greek and Latin. He wanted everyone to know about this humiliation and ridicule.

INRI are the initials in Latin for *"Jesus Nazarenus Rex Iudaeorum"* which translates to *"Jesus of Nazareth, King of the Jews."* Tradition states INRI was written on the sign above the head of Jesus on the cross.

Initials formed out of cruelty, ridicule, and disrespect. God takes all our broken names and shapes a new identity for each of us. Initials formed out of meaning, acceptance, and love

Image: Your Initials

Question: What are your initials and how have they shaped your life?

Prayer: God of all mankind, thank you for taking our messes and brokenness, and making us whole. May Jesus of Nazareth rule in our hearts forever.

Herod

*On hearing this, Pilate asked if the man was a
Galilean. When he learned that Jesus was under
Herod's jurisdiction, he sent him to Herod, who was
also in Jerusalem at that time.
When Herod saw Jesus, he was greatly pleased,
because for a long time he had been wanting to see
him. From what he had heard about him, he hoped
to see him perform a sign of some sort. He plied him
with many questions, but Jesus gave him no answer.
The chief priests and the teachers of the law were
standing there, vehemently accusing him. Then
Herod and his soldiers ridiculed and mocked him.
Dressing him in an elegant robe, they sent him back
to Pilate. That day Herod and Pilate became
friends—before this they had been enemies.
Luke 23: 6-12*

In recent years, the most popular baby names for boys
were Jackson, Aiden, and Lucas. You don't hear too
many parents naming their newborn Herod.

But in the Bible around Jesus' time and in the events
encompassing Jesus' life, the name Herod arises
often. Did you realize how many Herods lived during
this time? I think I need a clear pedigree chart to
figure this confusing family tree.

For example, Herod the Great is the father of the
Herod we read about in today's Bible verses. Herold
the Great is the king we hear about in the Christmas
Story – the one the Magi visited. The one who
murdered all the babies. He is the patriarch of this
family lineage.

Then Herod Archelaus comes along. When the angel
in a dream tells Joseph to bring Mary and Jesus back
home from Egypt, he is advised to go to Nazareth

instead of Bethlehem because of the threats and wickedness of Herod Archelaus.

Another Herod rule the area north and east of Galilee too. Herold Agrippa II appears in the trail of Paul in the book of Acts.

The Herod at the time of Jesus' trial is Herod Antipas. He is also the same man who killed John the Baptist, Jesus' cousin. This Herod divorced his first wife, married Herodias, the wife of his brother, who was yet a different "Herod."

Crazy family name, right? And not a wonderful family to name a child after, would you say?

Herod Antipas represented this family name well in his cruelty and mocking of Jesus. He wanted to see Jesus perform like a monkey in a circus. *"Show me a miracle, Jesus. Come on and do a trick to entertain me."*

Herod even dressed Jesus in an elegant robe – making fun of his kingship. Then Herod finished with his belittling of Jesus, before sending him back to Pilate.

Now Pilate and Herod shared something in common and became friends. They mutually used their power and influence to deride, use, and crush another to boost their own ego and self-interest.

Family names not only carry our identity, but also a connection to others. Our actions say something about what type of person we are and reflect onto an entire family. In Herod's family, evil, scorn, and sarcasm dominated their behavior.

As we hear the voices of this sadistic family, think about your family name, and the message and legacy left with its memory.

Image: Family Tree

Question: When others hear your name, what do they think?

Prayer: Lord of all, you continue to teach us lessons, even in the family trees of those who fail you. Help us to learn to be kind, generous, and loving to all we meet.

Interruptions of God

*A certain man from Cyrene, Simon, the father of
Alexander and Rufus, was passing by on his way in
from the country,
and they forced him to carry the cross.*
Mark 15: 21

Many of us want to spend more time with God. We
have good intentions. We start out strong, but after a
few days, or changes in schedules, or sick kids, or life
in general, we forget/postpone/purposely choose to
delete spending precious moments with God.

I believe God understands this common human
dilemma, but I sincerely want and desire to spend
more time with him.

We don't make time; we have difficulty in managing
time. We have no control over time or the disruptions
in life. Life happens. Things break. Outside
circumstances interfere. Unexpected sickness
unsettles our carefully planned day.

Since we cannot control interruptions, how to make
the best use of them? What lessons do interruptions
teach us? Our job is not to whine about life not being
fair, but in faith, return to God with an open heart,
willing to share our life with him.

In reflection, I find many interruptions hold meaning
in what they teach me and how they draw me closer
to God.

Simon from Cyrene came to town one day with his
two young sons. He was "passing by," minding his
own business, but Simon landed in the wrong place at
the wrong time.

People jammed the narrow streets of Jerusalem. They watched a man dragging a heavy wooden crossbeam. He struggled, obviously weakened by beatings, exhaustion, and despair. Jesus needed help.

Roman soldiers drafted Simon from the crowd. Perhaps Simon appeared strong. Maybe Simon's expression conveyed concern for the broken man before him. We don't know why Simon was picked, but his life changed in that instant by an interruption.

The transferring of the cross' weight from Jesus' shoulder onto Simon's brought them into intimate contact with one another. Simon must have looked deeply into Jesus' eyes and saw love.

What happened to Simon from Cyrene after that fateful day? Tradition tells us he became a follower of Jesus. The intimacy of walking with someone in their suffering leaves a deep mark on your soul.

I imagine Simon stayed at Golgotha, watching Jesus on the cross. Simon heard Jesus' final words. He probably met other followers there. Perhaps he lingered longer in Jerusalem and experienced the resurrection.

Allow interruptions to be God-moments. I used to get so perturbed with disruptions in my schedule. Now I hold them more lightly, allowing God to use them for his purpose, not cling to time just for myself. The intrusion may be unexpected for me, but not for God.

Listening and being with someone who needs us is vastly more important than our to-do lists. Interruptions can be tender moments where love is revealed.

Image: Cross

Question: What have interruptions taught you?

Prayer: God of every moment, open our eyes to the gift in interruptions. Give us patience and wisdom to know you are in control of our time and help us serve you in all the planned and disrupted minutes of our lives.

The Centurion

With a loud cry, Jesus breathed his last.
The curtain of the temple was torn in two from top
to bottom.
And when the centurion, who stood there in front of
Jesus, saw how he died he said,
"Surely this man was the Son of God!"
Mark 15: 37-38

A fireman saves a young child.
A nurse works an extra shift to provide care
A teacher spends an extra afternoon a week, helping a
student with his math.

Most of these people will tell you, *"I am only doing
my job."* Only? This is your calling. This is your job.
Your vocation is important. Lives are being changed.
These interactions transform and deeply affect
another human being.

Do the work God has given you and God will work
through you in amazing ways.

The centurion who served at Jesus' crucifixion was
also *"only doing his job."*

A centurion was a Roman office in charge of 100
soldiers. Roman soldiers stood guard at these death
sentences to control the crowd and carry out the
execution. The one in charge, the Centurion,
supervised from his spot, front and center to the
event.

The Centurion's job involved being watchful, in a
detached, impartial observation. His eyes scanned the
faces of those weeping at the foot of the cross. He
listened to the words exchanged. He scrutinized and
analyzed the details for his final report to his
superiors.

Don't you wonder what the Centurion thought? Today's verses reveal his final impression as he observed Jesus. The Centurion watched Jesus talk to the other criminals on each side of him. He saw the compassion expressed by caring for his mother's future. He witnessed the moment of incredible forgiveness radiating from a dying man.

The Centurion discovered love.

He confessed to those present, *"Surely, this man was the son of God."*

The Centurion's job was to observe and take notes. His work was to watch and he saw God at work. The cross of Jesus changes individuals.

Our *"just a job"* appears routine and trivial at times, but unexpectedly may reveal deeper meaning.

Do the work God has given us, then watch God work. Lives will be transformed. Love will be revealed. And even a Roman soldier's eyes will be opened and will see the truth.

Image: A nametag from work or something that symbolizes your calling.

Question: Where do you see God at work in your calling?

Prayer: Lord of all vocations, you call each of us to fulfill the work before us. Open our eyes to see your powerful transformation in the work of your hands.

Jesus, Remember Me

Two other men, both criminals, were also led out with him to be executed. When they came to the place called the Skull, they crucified him there, along with the criminals—one on his right, the other on his left.
One of the criminals who hung there hurled insults at him: "Aren't you the Messiah? Save yourself and us!"
But the other criminal rebuked him. "Don't you fear God," he said, "since you are under the same sentence? We are punished justly, for we are getting what our deeds deserve. But this man has done nothing wrong."
Then he said, "Jesus, remember me when you come into your kingdom."
Jesus answered him, "Truly I tell you, today you will be with me in paradise."
Luke 23: 32-33, 39-43

Jesus, remember me.

Words from a criminal crucified with Christ.

Words from a haunting Taize chant.

This slow peaceful tune sung on Good Friday, at funerals, or during worship provides comfort; the words, a sacred peace.

"Remember Me" is a song of hope.

Remembering gives us markers for our life's journey. Retelling our story adds meaning. We find God in our ordinary details and see his presence even in our difficult times.

We remember we are beloved children of God.

We remember Jesus' suffering, death, and glorious resurrection.

A deep cry from each of us to Jesus, *"Remember me."*

Remember me becomes our breath prayer. A plea for God to take us into his heart, never forgetting who we are and that we belong to him.

The phrase *"remember me"* implies a mutuality; an energy flowing back and forth between two beings. Jesus reminded us at the Last Supper, to "do this in remembrance of him." We are to hold sacred Jesus' life, his sacrifice, and his gift of love.

We remember Jesus. In turn, we ask him to remember us — a divine communion between two lovers.

During dark difficulties, we may not know how to pray. We struggle to find the words to express our need to God. All we want is to know he is here and knows our tears. At those times, a simple prayer like "Jesus, remember me" calms, comforts, and encircles us within God's care.

Jesus, remember me.

Image: A string tied around your finger, or a sticky note to help you remember.

Question: How do these words bring you comfort?

Prayer: Remembering Lord, we know you understand, accept, and love us. Help us recall your goodness and turn our hearts ever to your presence.

Keeping Vigil

Near the cross of Jesus stood his mother, his
mother's sister, Mary the wife of Clopas,
and Mary Magdalene.
John 19: 25

My dear friend, Esther, was dying. She lived 99
healthy and independent years, but those last five
months, I watched life slowly fade from her eyes.

I sat by her side. As the hours passed, her breathing
lightened and eyes rarely opened. I prayed. I held her
hand. I talked to her as if she would wake up and
smile. Most of the time, I just gazed at her face,
savoring the time together.

I was keeping vigil.

Near the cross, the women who loved Jesus also kept
vigil.

The phrase *"keeping vigil"* means to watch and
guard, and derives from the Latin word *"vigilia,"*
originally for a soldier's night watch. It is a time of
intense attentiveness to the present and to the
presence of God.

We watch as God watches with us. We keep vigil to
the One who always keeps vigil for us.

Keeping vigil contains an element of waiting. Not the
fidgety waiting in the line at the grocery store or the
impatience of begin snarled in slow moving traffic,
but a sacredness of holding time.

Remaining with Esther those last precious hours
became holy waiting, anticipating a great mystery as
life passes onto eternity.

The women at the cross stayed. They remained. They kept awake, clinging to Jesus words, listening to his breathing, and accompanying him on his final human journey.

Lent is a time for keeping vigil. We listen to the voices from Jesus' last week on earth, and we take them into our hearts, allowing their stories to form our stories.

We watch the mystery of Jesus' sacrifice and love, and wait for lessons to emerge. Wisdom that transforms our lives to become as God created us.

We pay attention to where God is moving in our lives and we follow. We become spiritually awake and alert to his presence in all we do.

We stay at the cross. We remain. We cling to Jesus' words and accompany him on his final human journey. We know he will walk with us on our final human journey, too.

We keep vigil.

God keeps vigil, too. A vigil over each of us.

Image: Light a candle.

Question: What are you learning during this time of keeping vigil during Lent?

Prayer: Thank you Lord for watching over us day and night. As we learn to wait, surround us with your presence to welcome the sacredness of keeping vigil.

Joseph of Arimathea

It was Preparation Day (that is, the day before the Sabbath). So as evening approached, Joseph of Arimathea, a prominent member of the Council, who was himself waiting for the kingdom of God, went boldly to Pilate and asked for Jesus' body. Pilate was surprised to hear that he was already dead. Summoning the centurion, he asked him if Jesus had already died. When he learned from the centurion that it was so, he gave the body to Joseph. So Joseph bought some linen cloth, took down the body, wrapped it in the linen, and placed it in a tomb cut out of rock. Then he rolled a stone against the entrance of the tomb.
Mark 15: 42-46

Different saints and spiritual teachers from history associate with different occupations and vocations. Some faiths believe these people serve as advocates for someone employed in that industry.

For example, Joan of Arc is assigned to protect soldiers. Fishermen look to Peter the Apostle. St. Augustine belongs to theologians and beer brewers.

I have always liked St Anthony of Padua who links with people or something that is lost. The delightful prayer to say when we can't find what we have lost is this: *"Tony, Tony turn around, something lost must be found."*

The patron saint of funeral directors is today's voice: Joseph of Arimathea. He is the person mentioned in all four gospels as the one responsible for the burial of Jesus. He was Jesus' undertaker.

Matthew describes him as a disciple of Jesus, and in today's reading we learn he is a *"prominent member of the Council"* which is the Sanhedrin. Luke 23:50–

56 adds he *"had not consented to their decision and action."*

The word that stands out to me though is he went "boldly" to Pilate. He probably hid the fact he followed Jesus as that would put him at risk, yet he knew he could and had to do something to care for Christ.

Under Roman law, the bodies of those crucified were left for vultures, adding further indignity and shame to the execution. The Jewish people didn't allow criminals to be buried in their family tombs as the criminal's presence would defile the others buried there. Often those bodies were taken to sites outside of Jerusalem.

The story of Joseph of Arimathea conveys a certain tenderness. The risky act of asking for Jesus' body. He wrapped Jesus' body in linen, gently placing it in the tomb. He rolled the stone against the opening to protect Jesus' body.

A friend who works for a funeral director told me once, she talks to the deceased person as she prepares them for the viewing in the casket.

"I ask them if they want their hair a certain way. I tell them I like the color they are dressed in. I treat them with respect."

This friend is acting like the patron saint for that person. She advocates for them, caring for their needs, gently cherishing them, and loving them.

I wonder if Joseph talked with Jesus as he prepared him for the tomb. Joseph advocated for Jesus boldly by asking for his body. He cared for Jesus' body with the burial preparation, and then protected him by rolling the stone before the entrance.

God invite us to advocate and protect others, too.

Image: A memento from a funeral or a piece of white linen

Question: Who is God inviting us to advocate for, care for, and protect?

Prayer: Lord of the living and the dead, you show us through your ongoing love how to care for others each day. Stir up within us a sense of being advocates for those in need.

Bring the Spices

Nicodemus, who had at first come to Jesus by night, also came, bringing a mixture of myrrh and aloes, weighing about a hundred pounds.
They took the body of Jesus and wrapped it with the spices in linen cloths, according to the burial custom of the Jews. Now there was a garden in the place where he was crucified, and in the garden there was a new tomb in which no one had ever been laid. And so, because it was the Jewish day of Preparation, and the tomb was nearby, they laid Jesus there.
John 19:38-42

If Joseph of Arimathea is the funeral director, his assistant is Nicodemus. Nicodemus brings the myrrh and aloes – the needed spices to best prepare Jesus' body for burial.

Earlier in John's gospel, we first meet Nicodemus who comes to Jesus at night and in secret to learn from him. Later in John, chapter 7, we read of his attempt to defend Jesus with the Pharisees.
"Nicodemus, who had gone to Jesus earlier and who was one of their own number, asked, "Does our law condemn a man without first hearing him to find out what he has been doing?"

Now he reappears with Joseph from Arimathea and assists in Jesus' burial. Embalming bodies occurred in different ways in different cultures. The Hebrews traditionally used spices and fragrant ointments. Nicodemus brought these supplies.

Were Nicodemus and Joseph of Arimathea heroes? They were ordinary men who followed their faith and acted in kindness and compassion. Love sometimes takes courage, but even a small gesture of compassion shines in significance to the one on the receiving end.

Life often races out of control. Most of us cannot change the course of history. We won't win Nobel peace prizes for negotiating the end of a major war between two countries. We won't discover the medication that cures cancer or heals Alzheimer's. People won't remember our work changed the course of the planets or stop the pollution of our air and waters.

But we can care. We can do simple acts of kindness. We help with the job others don't want to do, like burying a criminal.

We bring the spices.

Image: Spices or scented hand lotion

Question: Where is God calling you to act in kindness?

Prayer: Merciful God, open our eyes to see those around us in need. Let our hearts be broken by what breaks your heart, so we can best serve you by helping others.

Obstacles at the Tomb

So give the order for the tomb to be made secure until the third day. Otherwise, his disciples may come and steal the body and tell the people that he has been raised from the dead. This last deception will be worse than the first."
"Take a guard," Pilate answered. "Go, make the tomb as secure as you know how."
So they went and made the tomb secure by putting a seal on the stone and posting the guard.
There was a violent earthquake, for an angel of the Lord came down from heaven and, going to the tomb, rolled back the stone and sat on it. His appearance was like lightning, and his clothes were white as snow.
The guards were so afraid of him that they shook and became like dead men.
While the women were on their way, some of the guards went into the city and reported to the chief priests everything that had happened
Matthew 27: 64-6; Matthew 28: 2-4, 11

The security around Jesus' tomb was immense. Joseph rolled a large stone before the entrance. Pilate ordered guards to stand watch. No one could get past. No one would be able to steal Jesus' body.

Pilate wanted everyone to be done with this man, Jesus. He was dead.

As an extra precaution, Pilate ordered a seal be placed on the stone. The seal was a sign of authentication the tomb was occupied and the power and authority of Rome stood behind the seal. Anyone found breaking the Roman seal would suffer the punishment of an unpleasant death.

Before sealing the tomb, the guards were first required to inspect the inside of the tomb to be sure the body of Jesus was still there. After guaranteeing the corpse was where it was supposed to be, they rolled the stone back in place and sealed it with the official seal of the governor of Rome.

Roman seals were composed of a soft, moldable substance like clay. Imprinted on the clay was the Roman imperial seal and ropes attached to the stone.

Armed guards kept watch. The large stone blocked the doorway. Ropes and the seal provided further security. All this was extra measures to prevent someone from stealing Jesus' body. Many obstacles came between the outside world and Jesus. Barriers to keep the order; to maintain and keep life as it always has been.

All the precautions available in the world won't deter God. God has other plans. You can't constrain God. Obstacles won't stop him. God is more. God is always more.

God takes away the obstacles standing between us and him. Barriers erected by the outside world and hurdles we form from our fears and ego, nothing prevents God from coming to us and taking us into his heart.

God places his protection around our faith and our life. He seals our soul with his mark. He protects our heart with the guards of thankfulness, strength, and his Holy Spirit. God. God rolls away the large stone blocking us from entering his eternal presence.

Which obstacles will you choose? The world's or God's?

Image: A stone or seal

Question: What obstacles are in your way to draw closer to God? Which is bigger, your obstacle or God?

Prayer: Mighty God, we bow down in amazement at your determination to save each of us. Thank you for removing the barriers between us and reminding us nothing stops your love.

He Knows Our Name

Now Mary stood outside the tomb crying. As she wept, she bent over to look into the tomb and saw two angels in white, seated where Jesus' body had been, one at the head and the other at the foot. They asked her, "Woman, why are you crying?" "They have taken my Lord away," she said, "and I don't know where they have put him." At this, she turned around and saw Jesus standing there, but she did not realize that it was Jesus. He asked her, "Woman, why are you crying? Who is it you are looking for?"
Thinking he was the gardener, she said, "Sir, if you have carried him away, tell me where you have put him, and I will get him."
Jesus said to her, "Mary."
She turned toward him and cried out in Aramaic, "Rabboni!" (which means "Teacher").
Jesus said, "Do not hold on to me, for I have not yet ascended to the Father. Go instead to my brothers and tell them, 'I am ascending to my Father and your Father, to my God and your God.'"
Mary Magdalene went to the disciples with the news: "I have seen the Lord!" And she told them that he had said these things to her.
John 20: 11-18

He knew her name.

Mary arrived at the tomb and found it empty. She cried thinking someone has stolen Jesus' body. All she wanted to do was to care for him in the most proper and loving way.

Mary jumps to the wrong conclusion. What she sees with tear-filled eyes, and thinks with grief-filled emotions, blur the reality of the resurrection. Human perception presumes only a small portion of God's perspective.

Aren't we all like Mary? We don't see the full picture of God's kingdom plan. We think God isn't working fast enough, or not fixing our problems how we think best. We hold broken pieces and can't imagine the final mosaic masterpiece.

We don't always recognize God's presence even when right before our eyes. We miss seeing Jesus because we expect him to appear as we assume. We fail to experience his touch by fretting about what is wrong, instead of focusing on his promises of hope.

Jesus knew her name. Mary.

The sound of her name from her Lord and Savior dried her tears and mended her heart. Hearing his voice, knowing his presence, brought her attention back to Christ. He knew her name and now she knows the truth.

What an amazing reality – Jesus, the one who died and now lives - knew Mary's name and knows our name too. He created us and loves us. He waits to draw us closer so our hearts beat as one.

I have engraved you on the palms of my hands.
Isaiah 49: 16

Listen for Jesus saying your name. He is calling. He is present.

He knows your name.

Image: Birth tag from a hospital's bassinet

Question: What does Jesus call you?

Prayer: Dearest Lord, we can't find the words to express the wonder of how much you love us, want to be with us, and that you know each of us by name. Such intimacy. Such communion. Amazing love.

Thomas

*Now Thomas (also known as Didymus), one of the
Twelve, was not with the disciples when Jesus came.
So the other disciples told him, "We have seen the
Lord!"
But he said to them, "Unless I see the nail marks in
his hands and put my finger where the nails were,
and put my hand into his side, I will not believe."
A week later his disciples were in the house again,
and Thomas was with them. Though the doors were
locked, Jesus came and stood among them and
said, "Peace be with you!" Then he said to
Thomas, "Put your finger here; see my hands.
Reach out your hand and put it into my side. Stop
doubting and believe."
Thomas said to him, "My Lord and my God!"
John 20: 24-28*

I believe the Apostle Thomas gets a bum rap. Just
imagine being known for centuries by a derogatory
nickname – Doubting Thomas. This designation gives
the impression that doubting is wrong and something
we shouldn't do. The word implies if we doubt, we
are second rate, not good enough, failing in our faith.

But doubting - the process of questioning, explaining,
digging deeper, clarifying our faith - brings strength
to our roots and fruit to our branches. To cast aside
doubt trivializes the possibilities for growth in dry
seasons in faith.

Some faith traditions reject doubt and preach
something is wrong when you question. God isn't
afraid of your doubts. God wants you to come to him
with your questions. He loves having you near even
when skeptical.

Thomas endured a difficult time. His world turned upside down and he grieved a major loss. He needed some time to recoup. God understands the emotional turmoil we experience in life that breeds doubt, uncertainty, and hesitation.

Notice Jesus' response to Thomas. He doesn't criticize, shame, or punish him. Jesus simply offers Thomas a clear tangible action: Put your finger here. See my hands. Reach out. Do these things, and then believe. Jesus shows Thomas his wounds. He invites us to experience him in a new way.

Faith first. Doubts fade.

Thomas' doubt emerges into a profound transformational declaration of faith. His heart explodes with the magnitude and depth of the realization who Jesus is. God himself is standing right before his eyes. Jesus is Lord and God. He accepts Jesus' invitation to be with him and experience him. His honesty and his reaction gives us hope.

Faith first. Doubts fade.

The world can wear us down. In life, we confront discouragement, grief, and difficult circumstances. It is okay to admit this struggle to God. At times praying without words becomes the norm. We can sit silently, being with God, waiting in faith.

During Lent, ponder Jesus' wounds. Put your finger in his reality. See his life and his love for you.

God understands. He will at the right time show us the clear, tangible next step. It may be to attend church again. To read your Bible. To talk with your pastor or spiritual director. Maybe it is to find a retreat for some time away to walk, journal, and find yourself again. One step. One touch. On opportunity for you to put your finger on God once again, and believe.

Faith first. Doubts fade.

Image: A slip of paper with the words: Faith first. Doubts fade.

Question: What are the doubts you are currently dealing with, and how and where is this time of Lent inviting you to take one tangible step in faith?

Prayer: Thank you, Lord, for accepting and loving us even in times we are not sure and our eyes spill with tears of doubts. Show us the next step and will lead us closer to you and nourish our faith.

Come Along Side – Let's Walk Together

Now that same day two of them were going to a village called Emmaus, about seven miles from Jerusalem. They were talking with each other about everything that had happened. As they talked and discussed these things with each other, Jesus himself came up and walked along with them; but they were kept from recognizing him.
He asked them, "What are you discussing together as you walk along?"
Luke 24: 13-17

When I drive in my car, I like to imagine Jesus riding along with me – shotgun. I laugh since he should be driving the car – determining my direction, controlling my destination and steering this great adventure of life we are enjoying together. But that doesn't happen.

I talk with him. I smile at him. I tell him how I am feeling. We are companions and fellow travelers. Jesus and I become pilgrims, sharing this human journey.

The story of two people on the road to Emmaus is a favorite image of mine. Cleopas and another person stroll along on their way, talking about all that is happening in their lives. The shock of Jesus' death and now the rumors of his resurrection. Events moved swiftly and misinformation and fear overwhelmed them. What does this all mean?

Who comes alongside them? Jesus. Does he interrupt or preach at them? No, he unassumingly walks with them, asking questions as they go along the road. Jesus listens. He is present. He accompanies them in community and in love. He shares his word and his life with them, blowing the embers of their faith into a fire.

The story of the road to Emmaus experience is the story of our lives, too. We need companions to walk alongside of us. We need Jesus to be there, too. In this togetherness, we share our fears, experiences, faith, confusions, and doubts.

Like the two people heading to Emmaus, our world spins out of control, rumors and false news spread fear, and we shake our heads in disbelief in the occurrences around the globe. Daily announcements of mind-boggling, heart-wrenching terrorism overwhelm our faith and shatter our hope. What does this all mean?

We are all travelers on this road and Jesus comes along side us and walks with us. He listens. He is present. He accompanies and stays with us, building community and lavishing us with his love.

If we stay with Jesus, we will hear him as he shares his word and his life which will bellow the embers of our faith into fire.

We are the ones walking this road today. Jesus sits in the car next to us. Listening. Being present. Sharing his love and his life.

Image: A roadmap

Question: What does this all mean to you?

Prayer: Dearest Companion, thank you for sharing this journey with us. Walking beside us. Teaching us. Please continue to light our way and fan our faith so we see you and share your good news with others.

Back to Normal – Going Fishing

Afterward Jesus appeared again to his disciples, by the Sea of Galilee. It happened this way: Simon Peter, Thomas (also known as Didymus), Nathanael from Cana in Galilee, the sons of Zebedee, and two other disciples were together. "I'm going out to fish," Simon Peter told them, and they said, "We'll go with you." So they went out and got into the boat, but that night they caught nothing.
John 21: 1-3

When going through a tough uncertain time, where do you seek peace? Often we go back to what we know as a place for strength and nourishment for our spirit. We seek the familiar warmth of our comfort zones after an experience in the coldness of changing life circumstances.

Seven of Jesus' friends reacted the same way. They returned to their old normal. They decided to go fishing. They knew fishing. Fishing provided a predictable routine to sooth and comfort them. As a group, they stuck together. Misery loves company, right?

"I'm going fishing," Peter told the rest.

We'll come with you was their reply.

Yet, even the common act of fishing failed them this time. They caught nothing.

Ever go back to a place you left years ago? Maybe you return to your high school or a former place of employment. You walk the hallways. You pay attention to the chipped paint on the walls. Rooms seem smaller than you remember. But the worse feeling as you reminisce in that time capsule is you don't fit there anymore. You have moved on. This chapter has closed and you live in a new country now.

"Thanks for the tour, but I can't stay," you think as you scurry out.

Once you experience Christ and the powerful story of his love, you can't run back to the old normal routines. Routines bring comfort and provide a space to regain our perspective after a life changing experience. But after a short respite, it's time to start again. The old life becomes like fishing all night and not catching any fish.

Lent is an opportunity for reflection, reminiscing, and restoring. We walk through familiar stories. We hear the voices reliving the events of that week before Easter.

We know though, the tomb is empty. Jesus has risen. The power of the resurrection transforms us and invites us into new territory. The comfort zone loses its appeal and we hunger for more. For More.

The disciples returned to fishing – maybe to gain some perspective on all they experienced. But they, too, had been changed by the risen Christ. God had new plans for them which would take them far from what used to be normal.

The trouble with comfort zones is they are ruts of fear and exhaustion. Stepping away into the unknown takes courage. So does being a Christian – saying yes to Christ – and walking with him daily.

Jesus invites us on a new adventure. He comes to the edge of our routines and summons us to walk with him. He promises to stay with us, strengthening u, and guiding our way.

Leave the fishing nets behind and explore new territories with Jesus.

Image: A fishing net

Question: What new adventure is God calling you to?

Prayer: Lord of new life, we hear you calling. Thank you for staying with us as we step out of our ruts, our old normal, and into your adventure of life.

Come and Have Breakfast

*Early in the morning, Jesus stood on the shore, but
the disciples did not realize that it was Jesus.
He called out to them,
"Friends, haven't you any fish?"
"No," they answered.
He said, "Throw your net on the right side of the
boat and you will find some." When they did, they
were unable to haul the net in
because of the large number of fish.
Then the disciple whom Jesus loved said to Peter,
"It is the Lord!" As soon as Simon Peter heard him
say, "It is the Lord," he wrapped his outer garment
around him (for he had taken it off) and jumped
into the water.
The other disciples followed in the boat, towing the
net full of fish, for they were not far from shore,
about a hundred yards. When they landed, they saw
a fire of burning coals there with fish on it,
and some bread.
Jesus said to them, "Bring some of the fish you
have just caught."
So Simon Peter climbed back into the boat and
dragged the net ashore. It was full of large fish, 153,
but even with so many the net was not torn.
Jesus said to them, "Come and have breakfast."
None of the disciples dared ask him,
"Who are you?"
They knew it was the Lord.
John 21: 4-12*

Listen to the voice of Jesus. Hear how he talks with
his followers, his friends. He is friendly, not with
"holier than thou" churchy language. He does not
bellow from on high, looking down on his people. He
doesn't spout complicated theology with six syllable
words.

No.

Jesus asks, *"Friends, haven't you any fish?"*

Jesus simply beckons, *"Come and have breakfast."*

God prefers to talk to us as close friends. He asks Adam and Eve in Genesis, *"Where are you?"*

In Genesis 21, he asks Hagar, *"What is the matter?"*

God speaks directly and to the point to Paul on the road to Damascus, *"Saul, Saul, why do you persecute me?"*

We complicate our relationship with God. Fear confuses us. Sin obstructs us.

As we near Easter Sunday, listen for God's voice in the ordinary. Look closely at his created beauty in the center of a lily. Taste him in the flavors of jelly beans. Hear him in the giggles and voices of children. Sing with him with stirring music.

Walk in spring air – the birds use whatever voice God gave them to sing their praises. I like the Chinese proverb: *"A bird does not sing because it has an answer. It sings because it has a song."*

The trees burst their buds in regular cycles of the seasons. The world awakens from its winter slumber with primary colors and pops of pastels. Nature uses what it has and shares her gifts with the rest of us.

We, too, can use what we have learned this Lenten season – the voices and stories we read, the prayers that lingered with us, and lessons the Spirit unfolded in our hearts. Don't complicate the message.

I am a coffee morning person. I love to breath in the aroma and feel its steam on my lips. I sip its energizing liquid and feel it glide down my throat, waking every cell in my body. I smile and say, *"What some coffee, Lord? Join me as I read your word and listen to wisdom. "* I like to think he is sipping his coffee with me.

Simple interaction. Basic talk. Food among friends. Breakfast with the Lord.

God offers himself in straight forward, honest ways. I am here, he says. Come and have breakfast with me.

Image: breakfast items, such as cereal, toast or coffee.

Question: What do you hear Jesus saying to you?

Prayer: Thank you, Lord, for coming to us in uncomplicated, ordinary moments. We treasure the time we share together and the love you always give.

Our Calling

Then Jesus came to them and said, "All authority in heaven and on earth has been given to me. Therefore go and make disciples of all nations, baptizing them in the name of the Father and of the Son and of the Holy Spirit, and teaching them to obey everything I have commanded you. And surely I am with you always, to the very end of the age."
Matthew 28: 18-20

We've walked with Jesus through his last days on earth. We've listened and pondered the voices and experiences of those around him. We've seen both the good, the bad, and the human side of people. Not much different from our normal days, is it?

Jesus' last words are instructing us what to do next in the time after Easter. How should we spend our time until he comes again?

We are to go and bring others to God.

We are to baptize others, reminding all we are beloved children of God.

We are to teach and model obedience in all he commanded. He answered us earlier in his life about what is the greatest commandment. The one we are to keep front and center in our walk. The one essential instruction to guide all our thoughts and actions.

Love the Lord your God with all your heart and with all your soul and with all your mind. This is the first and greatest commandment. And the second is like it: Love your neighbor as yourself.

Perhaps Jesus' best parting gift is his last sentence. *"I am with you always."*

No matter where we walk.

No matter what we experience.

No matter what other voices we hear.

Jesus is with us always.

And of all the voices in our journey, Jesus' voice sounds the best.

"I am with you always."

Image: A key

Question: Whose voice are you going to listen to?

Prayer: Lord of all voices, thanks you for allowing us to listen to all the voices and their lessons heard on your last week on earth. Open our ears to recognize your voice and help us to follow your greatest commandments all our days.

Author's Notes

As I write this book, *40 Voices: A Lenten Devotional*, I soaked in the Scriptures, sat with the stories, and heard the voices from those around Jesus – yet it wasn't the Lenten season yet. What an honor to prep my heart early before embarking with Jesus to Jerusalem. I am so grateful for God's guidance and presence in his living word.

Lent is a wonderful time to reread the Gospels and imagine the scenes, the crowds, the emotions in all the voices. One some days, I would linger over the story and grieved at the cruelty shown to our Savior. Sadness overwhelmed my day.

Other days, I danced with hope and joy, knowing how much God loves his children.

Diving into God's words, then writing words from my own perspective opened a new depth and perspective of that day's reading for me. I encourage you to try this process too with your own devotions and prayers. Use your imagination. See, hear, taste and experience God's story.

Savoring the Scriptures will transform you and draw you closer to God.

If you enjoyed this Lenten devotional, I kindly ask that you leave a review on Amazon and other sites. I appreciate your support.

I have written additional books that are available on Amazon. You can find my author page at: healthyspirituality.org/amazon.

And please check out my blog: healthyspirituality.org. Let's connect there and on social media and continue our walk with Jesus together as children of God.

Made in the USA
Monee, IL
12 February 2020

21711705R00059